Yorkshire Bus Memories in Colour
By Paul Roberts

Copyright IRWELL PRESS Ltd.,
ISBN-10 1-903266-98-X
ISBN-13 978-1-903266-98-4
First published in 2008 by Irwell Press Ltd., 59A, High
Street, Clophill, Bedfordshire, MK45 4BE
Printed by Konway Press.

Introduction

In the first book in this series, *Midlands Bus Memories in Colour* (Irwell Press, 2007) I mentioned that I was brought up in Doncaster in the West Riding of Yorkshire, before moving to the West Midlands. Just over twenty bus companies operated stage carriage services into the town where they terminated at one of three different bus stations. This offered many different photographic opportunities. In my free time I often caught buses to nearby towns and cities and, where finances permitted, I would also take photographs of buses on these journeys. I occasionally travelled further afield with members of the Doncaster Omnibus & Light Railway Society (DO&LRS) to see and record less common buses and liveries.

This book is presented in the form of a tour of the three Yorkshire Ridings which existed until local government reorganisation in 1974. This seems an appropriate way of laying out my photographs as most of them were taken in the era of the West Riding, East Riding and North Riding. York, as the county town, was never in any of the Ridings and forms the final visit in my memories.

I attended Doncaster Grammar School, opposite the Christchurch bus station, and local Doncaster enthusiast Mick Fowler helped me to get part-time conducting jobs with Blue Line of Armthorpe and Reliance of Stainforth. When I was 18 I used to rush out of school and meet the 16.40 relief to Dunscroft, the driver (hopefully) having brought my ticket machine with him. I would then conduct the route, hoping that none of the teaching staff would number amongst my passengers! I also worked for Premier of Stainforth and on reaching the age of 21 they allowed me to take my PSV Drivers test, passed on Guy Arab IV YWX 644 which features in this book.

There are many well-known Yorkshire bus operators but by no means all of them are in this collection. *The Passenger Transport Yearbook* for 1968 lists almost 300 operators in England's largest county and this figure does not include major municipal and company fleets. Over 200 independents were based in the West Riding, 32 in the East Riding and 54 in the North Riding. This fact alone means that many have had to be omitted but I hope the reader enjoys sharing some of my favourites.

I would like to thank all who have helped me to remember some details of my own photographs! These include Paul Anderson, Dave Holt, Bob Palmer, Graeme Coles, Graham Frisby, Mike Greenwood, Bob Telfer, Simon Gill, Dave Mangham and Malcolm Danby, (with his fascinating memories of trolleybus driving in Bradford). My sister Jane assisted with early proof reading and, again, my wife Dot kept the whole project moving on when necessary.

Paul Roberts
Leicester 2008

Blue Ensign of Doncaster operated two AEC Regent Vs with Roe bodies. 758 NDT peeps out of its garage one Sunday morning in 1971 prior to taking up its duties on the service to Rossington, five miles to the south of the town. Doncaster was famous for the large number of independent operators running routes in the area. Until their steady demise started in the 1970s, over a dozen of these companies ran vehicles into the town's three different bus stations. Within a decade the majority had sold out and their colourful and varied liveries had all but disappeared.

It is a chilly Sunday morning on New Years Eve 1967. A group of enthusiasts from the Doncaster Omnibus & Light Railway Society has travelled to the Booth & Fisher depot at Halfway in the south-west corner of the West Riding. The group has arrived in the blue and cream Harrington-bodied AEC Reliance in the background, OUH 111, recently purchased by Premier (Coaches) of Stainforth near Doncaster. Both vehicles originally operated with Western Welsh and the opportunity has been taken to re-unite them over 200 miles from their original home. TUH 8, a 1960 Albion Nimbus NS3N with DP30F bodywork also by Harrington, is one of a total of eleven of these middle-size buses purchased by the company. They originally bought three, new in 1960, and liked them enough to get another eight from operators that included Great Yarmouth and Halifax Corporations. Their final Nimbus was also from Western Welsh, in 1968. The depot in the background was just five years old at the time of the photograph and would finally be closed down in 2007 by First in South Yorkshire, successors to South Yorkshire Passenger Transport Executive (SYPTE).

On Sunday 31 December 1967, WRA 12 is parked on Robin Lane, Beighton, at the junction of Manvers Road. This was the terminus for the Booth & Fisher route to Worksop that ran via Halfway, where the company was based and Wales, a local village. The bus is the second of a pair of unusual AEC MC3RV Monocoaches delivered in 1955 and fitted with Park Royal B45F bodies. This was a standard combination as the buses had no chassis and were of integral construction. The bus pictured here has survived into the 21st century and is now preserved at Rotherham as part of the South Yorkshire Transport Museum collection. The church on the left dates back to 1890 and bears the legend Primitive Methodist Church. The school on the right is notable for its completely open aspect. In common with all educational establishments it would be surrounded by security fencing in the years to come. Booth & Fisher operated until 1975 when they were taken over by South Yorkshire Passenger Transport Executive (SYPTE). For a short period the garage was kept separate from the other SYPTE operations, and their old livery continued on the all single-deck fleet until phased out in 1981.

These four Sheffield Corporation double-deckers are lined up at the back of Doncaster Waterdale bus station at the side of Glasgow Paddocks. They have all operated duplicate trips on the 77 route from their native city. Unusually they all belong to the A fleet that would not normally venture beyond the Sheffield city boundary. Out of town the C fleet, made up of vehicles that were wholly owned by British Railways, normally operated services. They have travelled the 18 miles to bring spectators to the Finningley air display in the autumn of 1967. In this period of strict regulation of services, the passengers would have to change on to the Leon service for the final leg of their journey. The nearest bus is a 30 foot long 1960 AEC Regent V 2D3RA, No.448 (7448 WJ) with a Weymann H39/30R body. Alongside is No.717 (RWJ 717), a Leyland PD2/12 also with a Weymann body but with H32/26R seating, dating from 1954. Next is a more unusual vehicle, No.763 (WWB 763) a 1956 AEC Regent III 9613S carrying another Weymann body but with an H33/25R layout. Sheffield Transport was the only operator to have AEC Regent IIIs with the style of 'tin-front' normally fitted to Regent Vs. A Roe-bodied Leyland Titan completes the line-up. Beyond them is a Doncaster Corporation AEC Regent V with a Roe body.

Alexander bodies were built in Falkirk, between Glasgow and Edinburgh. AEC Regent Vs with the Scottish-built bodies were mostly made for operators north of the border, so it was quite a surprise when Sheffield Transport purchased a batch of twenty vehicles with this chassis and body combination. They belonged to the wholly corporation-owned A fleet and No.373 (7873 WJ) with its H38/32R body is driving down Pinstone Street past Sheffield Town Hall, a magnificent Victorian neo-Renaissance building completed in 1896. Plenty of shoppers are out and about enjoying the sunshine though most prefer coats on the crisp afternoon of 14 May 1966. It will also be noted that several of the ladies are wearing headscarves and at least one appears to have left in her curlers in readiness for her Saturday night out! This was the era of shopping bags rather than disposable carrier bags.

It will have been a long time since the vehicle on the left carried workers to the Yorkshire Engine Company as shown on the destination display. BET 354 is a pre-war Bristol L5G dating from 1938. The bus was built with a B32C body at Cravens Coachbuilders in nearby Sheffield. All is not as it first seems in this 1968 view. Careful inspection will show daylight through the rear of the bus as it had actually been converted into a lorry for Rotherham Corporation Transport Department in 1955. This accounts for the non-standard red livery and fleet number SP1 (Snow Plough 1). Pre-war Bristols were fitted with PV1 radiators that were very high, permitting the driver a very limited view through a tiny windscreen. The lower PV2 post-war radiator is fitted to FET 805 on the right, allowing a direct comparison. It was No.105 until conversion to a driver-training bus, but has retained the standard fleet livery. It is one of twelve Bristols with East Lancs Bridlington H30/26R bodies delivered in 1949/50 and was an odd K6B among eleven other KS6Bs. Surprisingly, East Lancs built bodies in the Yorkshire seaside town of Bridlington from 1950-1953, following the take-over of the Yorkshire Equipment Co. Ltd. The depot in the background was Rawmarsh Road which once housed the Rotherham trolleybus fleet. The saw-tooth roof clearly shows the 'north lights', fitted to allow maximum light into the building. In 1984 the fleet moved to brand new premises in Midland Road, Rotherham. The old building and yard are still in use in 2008 as a storage and distribution depot.

There was a fashion for bus stations covered by multi-storey car parks in the Don Valley, starting with the two in Doncaster in the late 1960s and followed by this one in Rotherham. Whilst giving a degree of shelter from the elements to intending passengers, they also created a chilling wind tunnel effect on anything but the calmest of days. Photographers, used to patrolling open bus stations, had to wait for interesting buses to appear on departure, as is the case in this view in 1973. Rotherham Corporation Transport No.172 (WET 172L) is a rear-engined Seddon RU with an unusual choice at that time for a municipal operator, a 44-seat Plaxton body. It is carrying a style of fleet name over the coat of arms that was only used in the early part of the 1970s, before take-over by SYPTE in 1974. It is passing a well-loaded Daimler Fleetline, one of many bought by the department between 1967 and 1973. In the background is the heavy industry that was so markedly close to the town centre. The pub with the red sign is dispensing 'Wards Malt Ales' from a Sheffield brewery that was to close down in 1999.

A&M Foster Ltd was based at Dinnington their depot being mid-way between Sheffield and Worksop. On a miserable day in 1972 a second-hand AEC Bridgemaster 2B3RA with Park Royal H43/27F bodywork is parked outside in the depot yard. The unusual 'open-book' fleet name can clearly be seen forward of the rear wheel on the ex-Rotherham Corporation bus. It would be used mainly on contract services so the destination blind has been painted over and replaced with the simple legend 'FOSTERS'. Rotherham surprised local enthusiasts with its change to AEC double-deckers following several years of Daimler purchases. This bus was originally Rotherham Corporation Transport (RCT) No.140 (YET 940) and gave the transport department 11 years of service from 1961 to 1971 before making the short journey to its new home in Dinnington, where it joined other Bridgemasters from Rotherham and Leicester. Fosters, who also operated a stage carriage service from Dinnington to Kiveton Park, closed down in 1974. Following this YET 940 moved north of the border where it led something of a roving life. Within twelve months it was owned by Rennie's Lion and Comfort Coaches of Dunfermline, then Williamson's of Gouldry, both in Fife. Next it moved to Dougall of Dundee before going west to Gorman of Dunoon. In January 1975 it finished up, for two months or so, in the fleet of Harkins of Glasgow.

On a sunny day in the summer of 1971 a Bristol Lodekka has just inches to spare as it passes under Cudworth bridge heading from Pontefract to Barnsley. OWX 161 spent all its life in Yorkshire, being bought new by West Yorkshire Road Car in 1955. It ran for them as fleet No.DX17 for 14 years. By now it is in the fleet of Wrays of Hoyle Mill, a small independent that would be taken over by Yorkshire Traction in 1974. Until 1967 Wrays had operated this route jointly with Taylors of Cudworth and they traded as 'Ideal Service'. Low height buses were a necessity in this coal-mining area. A large network of railway lines criss-crossed the roads, many of them on bridges that did not allow the 14 foot 6 inch clearance required by normal highbridge buses.

Denaby level crossing is readily identifiable because of its acute angle. The road runs from Conisbrough to Mexborough and crosses the old Great Central railway line from Doncaster to Sheffield. Until 1961 Mexborough and Swinton (M&S) Traction Company trolleybuses had plied this route between Conisbrough and Rotherham. Conversion to diesel buses marked the end of the last trolleybus operation by the aptly named British Electric Traction group. In 1965 M&S bought JCD 29 and JCD 39 from Southdown Motor Services and operated them on their various routes. Rossie Motors of Rossington, near Doncaster, had for many years bought Daimler buses, so they surprised everybody by purchasing a pair of second-hand Southdown Leyland PD2s identical to the two running with M&S. It was inevitable that local enthusiasts would wish to re-unite these buses and on a grey 18 December 1966 that is what happened. JCD 51, formerly Southdown No.371, a 1948 all-Leyland bus with an H54R body, is on its way to the M&S Rawmarsh depot and has paused to allow passengers on the footbridge to record the scene. The Rossie buses had been bought specifically to operate school contracts and were not normally used on stage carriage service. Unusually for the company, they were never repainted in fleet livery.

In 1962 Mexborough and Swinton (M&S) operated a fleet made up in the main of 14 Leyland Atlantean double-deckers and 19 Leyland Tiger Cub single-deckers, all bought new. There was also a pair of ex-Southdown Motor Services 1939 Leyland TD5 double-deckers. This purchase began what was to become a steady stream of second-hand buses from Sussex to Rawmarsh, headquarters of M&S. By 1967 a total of 22 ex-Southdown vehicles had been in stock, although not all at the same time, including Leyland PD1s, PD2s and Royal Tiger coaches. In 1966 No.103 (OUF 834) joined the strength. It is a Royal Tiger built in 1955 with a luxurious Harrington C26C body and was a one-off with Southdown as their No.1834. The M&S livery was very similar to that of its previous owner and it is only the 'Mexborough' fleet name that confirms that it has moved to its new northern operator. Some vehicles, mainly double-deckers, carried the full 'Mexborough and Swinton' version of the fleet name. In this view at Rawmarsh depot, the rear of one of the aforementioned double-deckers can be seen at the top of the ramp. In 1969 when the National Bus Company was formed, M&S was soon merged with Yorkshire Traction, a much larger operator based eight miles away in Barnsley. The Rawmarsh depot, however, continued to be used by its new owners.

This is the old A1, better known as the Great North Road, just on the edge of Doncaster town centre. It is hard to believe that the opening of the A1(M) Doncaster by-pass was seen as a solution to the traffic problems in the town. Rossie Motors RYG 545L is the first of a pair of Roe H44/34F-bodied Daimler Fleetlines delivered in 1972. As was normal for the period the bus is full; in fact at peak times the only way to guarantee getting on board would be to get on at the bus station. It is half past the hour and the bus will follow the line of the old A1 for the first half of its journey before turning off into the mining village of Rossington. A quarter of an hour later the service will be provided by East Midland Motor Services, then Doncaster Transport on the hour and Blue Ensign at a quarter past the hour. At peak times it was normal for each operator to provide a duplicate bus for its own service. The bus stop is at Regent Square where the garden wall served as impromptu seating for generations of intending passengers. The combination of blossom and pedestrians wearing coats shows this to be the spring when, despite the sunshine, the days can remain chilly. The front of the Gaumont cinema is to be seen to the rear of the bus, soon after its conversion to three screens. In 1987, it would be renamed the Odeon, following the closure of its namesake 400 yards further down High Street.

In 1962 Rossie Motors purchased 220 AWY, a Roe-bodied H41/32F Daimler CVD6/30 which became something of a celebrity. Unlike twelve near-identical Gardner-engined buses, which would soon be running with nearby Doncaster Corporation, it was the last Daimler in the UK to be fitted with a Daimler CD6 8.6 litre engine. Few 30 foot buses were equipped with this power unit and, coupled as it was to a Daimatic 2-pedal control transmission, it made smooth, quiet progress, generating far fewer decibels than its Gardner-engined equivalent. When a second identical-looking bus BYG 890B arrived at Rossie in 1964, its louder sound effects soon confirmed that the more common option of a Gardner engine had been specified. This scene in April 1974 is at Coxley House, Rossington, at the depot which had been developed by W. Morpus in the 1920s and would go on to serve the company until it was taken over by SYPTE in May 1980. Along with BYG 890B and three Daimler Fleetlines, 220 AWY was taken into stock and continued in preservation for several more years. In common with many of the local independents, Rossie operated a few excursions, as can be seen by the board on the fence, where a trip to the Leeds-Derby match will cost a mere 35p. Rossie's coach 'fleet' comprised just two Duple-bodied Bedfords by this time and the Harper's Burlingham Seagull-bodied Guy UF in the background has brought visiting enthusiasts from the West Midlands.

Sandtoft Trolleybus Museum lies just over the county boundary in Lincolnshire. It is often associated with Doncaster, several of its volunteers living in that South Yorkshire town. The late Mike Dare and members of the Reading Transport Society had been looking for somewhere to house and operate their historic trolleybuses and the suitability of the old Sandtoft aerodrome persuaded them to set up their museum many miles from home. Other local enthusiast groups joined in and Sandtoft was born. Overhead wiring was erected round the circuit from the start of 1971 and the first trolleybus operated under the wires in 1973. Travelling round the circuit in the early days is Doncaster No.375 (CDT 636), a 1945 Karrier W now owned by the Doncaster Omnibus & Light Railway Society. It was re-bodied in 1955 with Roe H34/28R bodywork. Twenty similar bodies were converted to half-cab layout and transferred on to diesel chassis, giving many more years of service to this thrifty Yorkshire operator. No.375 is the only trolleybus driven by the author so it holds a special 'Yorkshire Bus Memory'! This scene is barely recognisable in the 21st century. The site is now home to dozens of trolleybuses in a setting of historic buildings and mature trees. The overhead wiring layout has been much expanded, comprising a two-way circuit and a variety of point-work and crossings.

In 1962 Doncaster Corporation Transport embarked on an unusual programme of re-using nearly new Roe H34/28R trolleybus bodies on diesel chassis. Over a two-year period this process was applied to twenty different buses. Six were transferred to ageing PD2/1s dating from 1947/8 and 1951 which had life-expired Leyland bodies, and two on to brand new PD2/40 chassis. Twelve new Daimler CVG6 chassis were also purchased and similarly treated. The first of these, No.168 (168 GDT) is heading along St Sepulchre Gate in 1972 on the only cross-town service in Doncaster. The 'lazy' destination display shows both of the outer termini and will be left in this position whether the bus is eastbound or westbound. Just to the left of the bus can be seen a large illuminated elephant over the entrance to the Elephant Hotel, and beyond that the familiar shape of a Burtons Tailors with the inevitable ballroom above. On the right are the first stages in the building of a brand new Arndale Shopping Centre.

Doncaster Corporation Transport was dedicated to AEC purchases from 1953 for a period of almost ten years. No.158 (XDT 158) is one of 31 lightweight AEC Regent Vs fitted with 7.7 litre engines and Roe bodies. It was built in 1957 and delivered in July but did not enter service until eight months later in March 1958. It seats 65 passengers in a bus which weighs only 6 tons 18 cwt – a remarkable achievement compared with buses in the 21st century, weighing in at well over 11 tons for hardly any increase in payload. The bus is actually heading towards the town centre on the Intake route, but the crew have already reset the destination for its next trip back to Leicester Avenue, a common custom in the town. The pub on the left, the Lonsdale, is notable in having a large building to the rear that regularly acted as a 'dormy shed' for a Lincolnshire Road Car Bristol Lodekka. The bus housed here would be used to operate the first and last service to and from Scunthorpe, 23 miles to the east of Doncaster. The car to the right of the bus is a BMC 1800 built at a time when this marque ranged across the products of Austin, Morris, MG, Riley and Wolseley. All the other cars visible are of British manufacture, not an uncommon sight during this period in the early 1970s.

Doncaster Corporation Transport (DCT) No.22 (MDT 222) is an AEC Regal III 9621A with a Roe B39F body. It was the first of a trio of identical buses delivered in 1953/54 making them some of the last half-cab single-deckers built in the UK. The Transport Department bought one underfloor engine AEC Regal IV in 1951, but it was not successful and the tried and tested combination of a vertical engine and crash gearbox was specified for Nos.22-24. The trio was purchased to operate the 77 route to Sheffield which included an arch of 11ft near Meadowhall, necessitating the use of saloons until a diversion was brought in, permitting double-deckers to operate this busy route. In 1958, all three underwent conversion, at C.H. Roe in Leeds, enabling them to be used as 'pay as you enter' buses. The hinged plate behind the front wing labelled them to this effect. The conversion involved placing a 45 degree angled window and counter, that can clearly be seen between the driving cab and the passenger entrance. The bus was adopted as a favourite by the late Les Flint, then chairman of the Doncaster Omnibus and Light Railway Society (DO&LRS) and was used on many DO&LRS excursions. DCT kindly kept it in service until 1972, seven years longer than No.23 and No.24, when it was placed on permanent loan to the Society. In 2003 the author was privileged to drive the bus on its 50th birthday party at Sandtoft, where DO&LRS continue to maintain it in excellent condition. The view is at DCT Leicester Avenue depot in 1970. It is alongside HBE 260, a pre-war AEC Regal, re-bodied with a 30ft long B39R Saunders-Roe body. It was originally operated by Enterprise & Silver Dawn but is with Premier of Stainforth. The wooden buttress to the right is part of an old hanger used to house municipal refuse wagons.

In common with most Yorkshire municipal fleets, Doncaster Corporation had for many years operated a fleet that was largely made up of double-decker buses. This was all to change in the mid-1960s when saloons made up 5% of the fleet. Several batches of single-deck buses were purchased from 1965, boosting this figure to 40% by 1972. One reason for this was that legislation of the time did not permit driver only operation of double-deck buses. Doncaster bought two batches of Leyland Royal Tiger Cubs which remained unique to this operator. This bus, No.1041 (FDT 41C) is one of the first batch of ten RTC1/1s, fitted with Leyland 0600 engines and synchromesh gearboxes, carrying Roe B45D bodywork dating back to 1965. The second batch of ten RTC1/2s had pneumocyclic semi-automatic transmission and a much more modern-looking Roe B45D body with single piece curved windscreen. The bus is in a hybrid condition, bearing its new PTE fleet number but still with the livery and fleet name of its former operator. It is outside the Art Deco Co-op Department Store in Printing Office Street. No.1068 (CDT 568H) behind is one of 14 Seddon RU buses fitted with Seddon Pennine B42D bodies and delivered in 1970. These were not totally successful and 11 more Seddons were bought in 1972 but this time with the undertaking's favourite Roe bodies. Both the buses are en route to destinations previously served by trolleybuses until their demise in 1963. The livery was very innovative for its time and the stripe was said to represent a road between two footpaths!

Doncaster Corporation Transport (DCT) bought its first 30 foot long double-decker in 1962 and a year later No.190 (190 NDT) heralded a second batch of six almost identical Roe H40/32F-bodied Leyland PD3/4s with traditional exposed radiators. In both years they also 'dual sourced' and bought a similar number of Daimler CVG6-30s, also with Roe bodies. These vehicles all survived into the era of the South Yorkshire Passenger Transport Executive (SYPTE). No.1190 was an early repaint into an experimental new livery that was intended to be unlike those of the three constituent fleets of Sheffield, Rotherham and Doncaster. They succeeded in producing this coffee and cream livery which certainly bore no resemblance to anything previously seen in the area, but was generally felt to be too insipid. A new, short-lived SYPTE logo can also be seen below the waist rail, and this would soon be replaced by a stylised SY between the decks. Route numbers had been abandoned by DCT in the 1950s but they were reintroduced in the early 1970s, only to have them all changed by the newly formed PTE! The bus is travelling down Town Moor Avenue in the autumn of 1974 en route to Lothian Road. If the SYPTE had followed its plans to introduce trolleybuses to the area, this route passing close by the Leicester Avenue depot would have become an early candidate for conversion to electric traction. However the politics of the 1980s intervened and the plans were dropped.

Sheffield Transport ordered a batch of 56 Daimler Fleetlines fitted with ECW H43/27D bodywork in 1973, shortly before the department was transferred to the South Yorkshire Passenger Transport Executive, on 1 April 1974. The body was built to a brand new design incorporating windows that clearly showed their origins. The front and rear roof peaks were a complete change from anything ECW had produced previously. No.783 (CWE 783N) is just the third one to be produced by the Lowestoft factory and is on a test drive soon after completion. The blue totem sign pointing to North Station refers to Oulton Broad, not a little-known Sheffield suburban station! Although the bus is carrying its new fleet number and registration it is travelling on a trade plate, which is visible inside the windscreen. A white-coated engineer can be seen alongside the driver, presumably assessing the brand new bus. By the time this batch was built in 1974/75 South Yorkshire PTE had inherited the order and they were all delivered in their newly developed livery. The only other buses to carry this design of bodywork were a small number of single-door Leyland Atlanteans bought by Colchester Borough Transport, also in 1975. Once in service a blind spot was identified behind the very thick corner pillars by the windscreen. Inserting a narrow triangular window below the wing mirrors rectified this problem.

Hexthorpe is a suburb of Doncaster, close to the famous Plant Works, as it was known locally, where many famous steam locomotives were built. Walkers of Hexthorpe operated a small but very smart fleet of buses and coaches but as they had no stage carriage services they were not as well known to enthusiasts as many other independents in the area. Their operation was licensed for express service and excursions and tours and they also operated contracts and private hire. They had two double-deckers and four coaches presented in this unusual red and grey livery. This combination of colours enhances the stark lines of 468 MTX, a Weymann H37/28F AEC Regent V. It started life with Rhondda Transport in South Wales in 1962 and was relatively new when it moved up to South Yorkshire at the end of the decade. Three miles from its Hexthorpe base, it is resting on the other side of the River Don in the Urban District of Bentley with Arksey. This area was to be in the national news following devastating floods in the summer of 2007.

Doncaster Christchurch was often called a bus station by locals but actually amounted to half a dozen terminal bus-stands round two sides of the churchyard. Having the excellent Cooplands Café and a public convenience opposite, bus crews and passengers alike had all the facilities they could wish for! Enthusiasts were catered for too as the historic church provided a fine backdrop for their photographs. Morgan and Store (Blue Line and Reliance) operated several services from Christchurch, all heading eastwards to Armthorpe, Stainforth, Thorne and Goole. On a Sunday in April 1974 7014 YG, a 1962 Roe H73F-bodied Guy Arab IV is loading for Goole, a town some 20 miles away. The bus carries a 'Johannesburg' front and was unique in the Doncaster area. A friend was asked to read the registration plate on his driving test in 1966 – a feat he could have completed even if the number plates had been removed! To the rear is WWX 671, another Guy Arab IV but with a traditional exposed radiator. The body is by Burlingham of Blackpool, as is the one on the single-decker. The author arranged the meeting of a pair of Burlingham-bodied Guys in conjunction with local enthusiast Mick Fowler. Having brought Harpers No.59 (1293 RE) to Yorkshire in the carefree days before log books and tachographs, both drivers were keen to swap steeds and unofficially enjoy the challenge of the different crash gearboxes on offer, as a tour of local operators continued.

Blue Line of Armthorpe bought a fleet of Guy double-deckers built up through the 1950s and 1960s, so the purchase of a pair of Roe H73RD-bodied Leyland PD3A/1s in 1968 came as something of a surprise. Kippax and District, near Leeds, originally bought them in 1965 so they must have represented a bargain when sold off a mere three years later. Illuminated advertisements on buses were in vogue in the 1960s and DUG 167C would eventually be fitted with a display for 'Blue Line Coaches'. As a stop-gap the original panels have simply been reversed to show a plain white expanse. It is a busy Saturday afternoon at Christchurch bus station in Doncaster. The bus is carrying a full load on the Armthorpe route, whilst many more passengers have formed an orderly queue for the service. Blue Line's sister company Reliance used Willebrew ticket machines. These involved clipping a chunk out of the ticket and paying in 'blind', as only the cash office could calculate the amount due, by counting the tiny off-cuts. The author has mixed memories of this ticket system. It was in use at the time he gained his PSV Conductors Badge in 1967. Clipping nearly 1,000 tickets in a shift on Friday, colliers payday, would tax even the most enthusiastic of employees; Reliance would issue a second ticket machine as the first one would inevitably fill up and jam.

Harold Wilson Ltd traded as Premier of Stainforth and ran 20-40% of the Doncaster to Thorne Moorends route, along with Severns and Felix. Five buses were required to maintain the 20-minute frequency, of which Premier always provided one on a permanent basis and a J (joint) service was provided by them for two weeks in eight. Along with a commitment to several colliery services and three-shift workings to Lysaghts steelworks in Scunthorpe, this provided plenty of employment for their fleet of half a dozen double-deckers and 15 coaches. Through the 1950s, they bought a number of Guy Arabs, all from new, of which YWX 644 was the only one with a front entrance. In 1965 Premier became the first independent in the area to buy a Daimler Fleetline in the form of a Roe H78F CRG6LX, HYG 123C, seen on the right of this depot yard view. XWU 798L was also new to them in 1973, but had an Alexander H74F body on a Leyland Atlantean AN68/1R chassis. The multi-coloured livery suits the angular shape of the Park Royal H43/28R-bodied AEC Bridgemaster, 310 MFC. City of Oxford Motor Services originally bought it in 1961 and after many years service it was sold in 1973 to Sheriff of Gainsborough (Star Services). That same year it moved the relatively short distance to Premier in Stainforth. In an attempt to cut down on excess tyre wall wear in the narrow streets of Thorne HYG 123C was, for a while, fitted with 'Super-Single' rear wheels. These were set further in than normal which helped the curbing problem but led to a degree of instability and a strange rolling motion often resulted (as experienced by the author when conducting the bus) so the experiment was discontinued. Premier continued operating until June 1988 when it became the last Doncaster independent bought by the SYPTE.

YWX 644 is a 1959 Roe-bodied H37/28F Guy Arab IV. In 1970 it was fitted with a Gardner 6LX 150hp engine to replace its worn out 6LW 112hp unit, giving it more than enough power for its quick jaunt along the M18 motorway. The bus, surprisingly, is on a stage carriage service between Doncaster and Thorne Moorends. When the motorway first opened it severed the direct A1146 road between Hatfield and Thorne until the new over-bridge was complete. This necessitated a somewhat unusual diversion, as we see. The motorway also saw rear-entrance open platform double-decker buses, something which would cause nightmares for operators in our modern health and safety era. The lack of traffic is notable. The area to the left of the island is now taken up with the large Doncaster North service area, strategically placed alongside the junction with the M180 to Scunthorpe and Grimsby. This bus was a particular favourite of the author, who passed his PSV test on it in 1970.

The firm of T. Severn and Sons operated to Dunscroft and Thorne Moorends from Christchurch, Doncaster. In the 1960s, bus crews would refer to the company as the 'Cressy' a fleet name which had officially been dropped during the war! All the double-deckers that were bought new from the 1950s onwards were Leylands, progressing from PD2s to PD3s and finally Atlanteans. The first Atlantean was delivered in 1965 and the second in 1969. The latter was unusually badged as an Albion Atlantean because it came through the Leyland works with a batch for Glasgow. South of the border, it remained unique. On take-over by SYPTE in 1979 they had built up a fleet of ten of these rear-engined buses and all were taken into stock and operated by their new owner. SWR 3L was the first of a pair delivered in 1972 with Roe H43/29F bodies. The bus is equipped for one-person operation, but would only be used as such off-peak. A conductress can be seen in this 1974 view as the bus makes its final approach to Christchurch bus station along Thorne Road, Doncaster. The midday sun has obviously had its effect, as the crew are happy to cool the bus down by driving along the main A18 road with the doors open. It is being pursued by a long wheelbase CF van, a Bedford attempt to compete with the much more successful Ford Transit.

T. Severn and Sons of Dunscroft near Doncaster was well known for its fleet of Leyland double-deckers most of which were bought new. A surprise purchase in 1964 was EPM 13, a 1949 Bristol K5G with the usual highbridge body associated with Brighton Hove & District, the original purchaser. (Severns also bought a London Transport RT, HLX 148, at about the same time.) It soldiered on for several years, mainly on duplicate journeys. With its crash gearbox and slow revving Gardner 7.0 litre, 5-cylinder engine, Severn drivers would not relish driving this bus, compared to their more usual 9.8 litre Leyland synchromesh steeds. The company also operated a small number of Albion and Scammell trucks. Some of these can be seen in this 1966 view. Severns were taken over by the South Yorkshire Passenger Transport Executive (SYPTE) in 1979. Their modern garage continued to serve SYPTE as their eastern-most depot for many more years.

Blue Ensign was one of the smaller operators to run a stage carriage service into Doncaster and it was the only one to be based in the town rather than in the surrounding villages. From the 1920s, the company formed by G.H. Ennifer had its garage in Bentinck Street but in 1968 moved to a brand new depot in Union Street/Cleveland Street. This was just a few hundred yards from the Southern bus station from where their service started. They ran a variety of second-hand buses in the 1950s but in 1959 3568 DT, a brand new Roe H41/32F AEC Regent V 2D3RA, was purchased. Five years later in 1964, its almost identical twin 758 NDT arrived.

These buses were always in immaculate condition, carrying gold-leaf lining and chromium plated wheel trims. The service to Rossington, a mining village five miles to the south of the town, took one hour for a round trip. The route was jointly operated with Doncaster Corporation, Rossie Motors and East Midland Motor Services who acquired their 25% share in the service when they bought out Don Motors in 1962. Blue Ensign bought a Daimler Fleetline in 1967 and another pair in 1975 that saw the demise of the magnificent pair of AEC Regents. In April 1978 the company was bought by SYPTE who closed down the garage and moved the fleet of three buses and three coaches to their Leicester Avenue depot, near Doncaster racecourse.

Felix Motors of Hatfield was well known for its immaculate buses running into Doncaster's Christchurch terminus. Two routes were operated, one to Thorne Moorends 12 miles distant, and the other to Armthorpe, a village just three miles away. In the summer of 1973, AEC Regent V No.42 (8176 WY) dating from 1961 and carrying a Roe H41/32R body, is just setting off from the terminus on its 45 minute round trip to Armthorpe. This route was jointly operated by Blue Line, Felix and Doncaster Corporation Transport. The famous Christchurch can just be seen on the extreme right. The background is dominated by the massive bulk of the Gaumont cinema that also occasionally hosted live acts, notably the Beatles in their early days. Lonnie Donegan recorded *My Old Man's a Dustman* here, a number one in the Hit Parade for four weeks in 1960. It went on to be the last Gaumont cinema in the UK when in 1987 it was renamed the Odeon. This caused some confusion to many Doncastrians as traditionally the junction of the two main roads at the front of the cinema has been called Gaumont Corner.

In the 1950s and 1960s, Leon of Finningley operated a varied fleet, but the majority of their double-deckers were quiet Daimler-engined buses. This all changed in 1966 when Devon General sold off a batch of 12 1954-built AEC Regent III 9613s fitted with Weymann H32/26RD bodies. Three of them found their way north to Leon's and made their presence known with their musical gearboxes and booming 'straight-through' exhausts. To the delight of local enthusiasts, these three Regents could be identified long before they could be seen as they roared through the town, unlike their more mundane counterparts operated by other local operators. On Saturday 22 April 1967 the bus is serving Wroot, a small village in Lindsey (Lincolnshire) just beyond Finningley. PDV 725 is actually travelling into Doncaster, having passed through three counties, Lincolnshire, Nottinghamshire and Yorkshire on its relatively short journey into town and the Southern bus station. Waterdale, behind the bus, is full of fascinating British-built cars but every afternoon would host a mass of Hall Bros. coaches taking a break on the Coventry to South Shields service. Attenborough and Beet's garage, on the left, has a very old-fashioned petrol pump below the *Fina* sign. Petrol was dispensed through a long arm which swung out over the footpath above the heads of pedestrians.

South Yorkshire Motors, based in Pontefract, operated several long distance stage carriage routes. They specified fewer seats in their buses than would normally be offered by the manufacturer in order to provide more comfort for passengers on these long journeys. No.88 (PWR 988E), a Leyland Atlantean PDR1/2 with Roe H70F body, is almost new when seen in Marsh Gate bus station in Doncaster on 10 August 1967. The extra leg room will be appreciated by any passenger making the full journey through to Leeds, a distance of 29 miles with a journey time of 1½ hours. No.88 would rarely visit Marsh Gate because soon after this photograph was taken, a new Northern bus station was opened much closer to the town centre. In 1973, South Yorkshire Motors became South Yorkshire Transport Ltd, just before SYPTE was formed, although there was little room for confusion with the independent's modernised blue and white livery. This famous livery finally disappeared before the turn of the century, following take-over by the Caldaire Group.

What a lot of traffic! The queue on the right is on the A18 Sheffield- Grimsby road through Doncaster in 1966, when it was not uncommon for such trunk routes to penetrate the hearts of our towns and cities. The students of Doncaster Grammar School for Girls (the copper dome of which can be seen to the right) suffered from the noise of the constant stream of lorries and buses passing through Waterdale. The rear end of Leon's Burlingham Seagull-bodied Daimler Freeline coach can be seen ahead of the three lorries. No.1082 (LHE 510) is a striking centrepiece having just been repainted by its owners, the Yorkshire Traction Company (YTC). It is based at their Milethorne Lane depot in the town, but is laying-over near their central office and canteen. It is one of 27 Leyland PS1 single-deckers, re-bodied by Roe in 1956 and 1957. Another YTC bus can be seen to the rear, one of many Leyland Tiger Cubs that they operated. Heath & Smith, soft drinks manufacturer, was a well-known name in the town which, in common with similar companies round Britain, used to bottle Guinness. This accounts for the advertisement on the back of their lorry, parked behind the double-decker. The church on the left was to become one of the first in England to be converted into a pub, a matter of great contention at the time.

The double-deck bus emerging from the gloom of Doncaster's Southern bus station is a Yorkshire Traction Leyland PS2 rebuild. It was originally a Yorkshire Woollen District single-deck vehicle, its body removed and replaced by a Northern Counties 63 seat double-deck body in 1963. There were several different routes from Doncaster to Barnsley but service 22 via Conisbrough and Mexborough was by far the busiest. This sighting of No.794 (YHE 243) is quite unusual on this autumnal day in 1967 because larger capacity PD3s were normally used on this route. The single-decker to the right is on the infrequent service to Scunthorpe that, even at this time, ran less often than the competing railway service. No.1207 (BVL 46C) is one of a pair of ECW B54F-bodied Bristol RE buses delivered to Lincolnshire Road Car in 1965. The bus station had only recently been opened but went on to give 40 years of service before replacement by a bus/rail interchange close by, in 2006.

'United Services' was a common fleet name used by three operators on a joint route from Doncaster to Wakefield. They were W.R. & P. Bingley of Kinsley near Hemsworth and Cooper Bros. and Everett, both of South Kirkby. Everett sold out to Bingley in 1969 and Cooper Bros. to Bingley in 1977, just a fortnight before Bingley itself sold out to West Yorkshire PTE! The whole route ran through pit villages criss-crossed by railways that made for many low bridges. The fleets thus included many 'lowbridge' double-deckers with up to 53 seats but the layout involved an offside upstairs gangway and four seats across, very awkward for the collection of fares. When longer single-deckers, up to 36 feet long, were permitted, it was possible to get the same number of passengers on one deck and so the United Services double-deckers were gradually ousted. SWT 704F is, unusually for an independent, a rear-engined AEC Swift MP2R with Willowbrook B53F bodywork, delivered in October 1967. It has just made its way down the hill from the historic village of Hooton Pagnell and has crossed over the trackbed of the old Hull & Barnsley Railway. Careful inspection shows that the bus is still 'crew-operated' as a conductress can be seen collecting fares at the back of the bus. In common with most AEC Swifts, the vehicle was found to be troublesome and was soon sold on. It ended its days with Berresfords of Cheddleton, Staffordshire where it was left to slowly rot in the field at the back of their depot with a host of other disused buses.

Many early rear-engined single-deck buses proved to be unreliable and something of a burden to their owners. In 1964, Manchester City Transport (MCT) purchased a batch of Park Royal B43D Leyland Panther cubs, a 33 foot long version of the Panther that was fitted with a relatively small 0400 engine with only 6.54 litre capacity. ANF 161B was the very first of a batch of 20 such buses that were underpowered and, with two doors, suffered from structural bodywork problems. As South East Lancashire North East Cheshire (SELNEC) Passenger Transport Executive buses they were soon sold on to other operators. ANF 161B went on to Coopers, part of the United Services combine, in 1971. Coopers managed to 'tame the beast' and found it quite successful. It passed to W.R. & P. Bingley in 1977, this company almost immediately coming under the ownership of West Yorkshire PTE. It is basking in the sunshine at its South Kirkby depot in this 1971 view and is proudly displaying its rare Panther Cub badge on the radiator grill.

Yorkshire was not only famous for operators but also for dealers and bus scrap yards. Even in the 21st century, the last journey for many a bus is to the breakers' yards of South Yorkshire. On a Sunday in March 1967, the author arrived at Ben Johnson's yard, outside South Elmsall, just in time to find an ECW bus being reduced to ashes. It is unidentifiable but does appear to be a lowbridge vehicle. In this era, all re-usable parts (the term 'recycling' had not been invented then) were removed. When the vehicle was just a shell it would be burned to reduce non-metallic components. Times change: in the 1960s it was quite acceptable to produce all the emissions consequent on the burning of the final body shell. Note also that the yard is alongside the main railway line from Doncaster to Wakefield and Leeds, subsequently electrified in 1991.

In 1972 the last of West Riding's ill-fated Guy Wulfrunians were withdrawn. As a result, a number of lowbridge bodied Guy Arabs continued in service longer than would otherwise be expected. The batch of 45 of these buses delivered in 1957 had platform doors to improve passenger comfort and safety. No.422 (KHL 819), originally No.819, a Roe H55R Guy Arab IV is waiting to return to Pontefract in the recently opened South Elmsall bus station. West Riding had, until 1969, been the largest independent in the country, but had now come under the umbrella of the National Bus Company, as had the Yorkshire Traction Company (YTC) bus behind. YTC had long been associated with Leyland products but in 1968 and 1969 they split an order for 14 rear-engined buses between Leyland Atlanteans and Daimler Fleetlines. No.658 (RHE 658G) is one of the 1969 Atlanteans and carries a fairly unusual Northern Counties H44/31F body with long 'panoramic' windows on its PDR1/3 chassis.

County Motors of Lepton was one of the smaller British Electric Traction (BET) companies operating from just one depot at Waterloo, on the eastern edge of Huddersfield. For many years Yorkshire Woollen District, West Riding and Yorkshire Traction (YTC) jointly owned this company. With a fleet strength of a mere 23 vehicles it was hardly surprising that the operation was absorbed into Yorkshire Traction soon after the formation of the National Bus Company in 1969. The West Riding influence meant County bought a pair of Guy Wulfrunians in 1962. The following year they had both moved to Wakefield to join the

several dozen similar buses already operated by West Riding. In 1964 a pair of much more conventional front-engined buses was bought by County, Nos.105 and 106 (AVH 635/6B) to replace the Wulfrunians. These were Roe H42/31F-bodied Leyland PD3A/1s and always stood out as being the only ones with handsome composite bodies in the YTC fleet. All the other PD3s bought by Yorkshire Traction with Roe bodies were to a Park Royal metal framed design. In 1969 when they became part of YTC, the buses lost their unusual cream and blue livery, to be painted into 'Trackys' red and cream. AVH 635B is YTC No.745 but prefers to remain anonymous when seen in Wakefield bus station, just behind a West Riding Bristol RE. It is still on its old County haunts, operating the 63 route to Huddersfield via Flockton and Lepton.

The sorry saga of the Guy Wulfrunian has been well documented but makes an interesting story, worth outlining here. Towards the end of the 1950s, Guy Motors of Wolverhampton designed a chassis (named after a native of its home town) which was full of innovation. It had air suspension, disc brakes and many other features unheard of at the time. West Riding Automobile were involved in the design and gave the end result full backing in the form of firm orders. Unfortunately after just a few years the buses proved to be very unreliable as many of the new features failed under the rigours of daily service. West Riding bought all but 11 of the 137 built between 1959 and 1965. The company subsequently purchased five of the remainder second-hand. Their rapid demise also saw the end of Guy Motors in

the 1970s. Charles H. Roe of Leeds provided bodies for almost all of these buses and a handful were first operated by West Riding in a red livery to denote that they were on the old tram routes to Leeds, abandoned in 1932. On a sunny summer day in 1969 No.955 (VHL 955) is loading in Wakefield bus station. The independent suspension has caused the front wheels to slope inwards, as is common to all these buses. Unusually the cab door is wide open to 180 degrees with bump-stops to protect the bodywork rather than a more normal restraining strap made of leather or canvas. In April 1967, in a desperate attempt to remove half a ton of payload from the front axle, the front upstairs seats for eight passengers were removed and horizontal bars placed across the front to prevent access. This bus was withdrawn after barely seven years in service, but some of the 1965 models saw only five years before being scrapped. Some of the Gardner 6LX engines were retrieved, and would be fitted in a batch of 1972 Daimler Fleetlines, new to the company.

When West Riding purchased over 100 modern Guy Wulfrunians, festooned with new features for the time, they would not have expected that, within five years of the newest ones being delivered, they would be in desperate need of replacement. West Riding had been the largest independent operator in the UK but in 1967 it sold out to the nationalised Transport Holding Company (THC). In 1969 this became the National Bus Company (NBC). Soon after, the NBC was able to arrange for the transfer of over 70 rugged and reliable Bristol Lodekkas to the West Riding fleet from other constituent companies. No.537 (EHU 584C) is one of many that moved from the Bristol Omnibus Company, where it was their No.7238. An FLF6LW with ECW H38/32F bodywork dating from 1965, it, too, is looking somewhat anonymous in its drab green livery without a fleet name. Immediately behind is another similar bus in its new NBC red livery, along with West Riding, its fleet name, in NBC corporate style. At the rear of the trio is one of over 100 Daimler Fleetlines bought between 1969 and 1972, this one having bodywork built by Charles H. Roe in nearby Leeds.

As noted opposite from 1969 West Riding received over 70 second-hand Bristol Lodekkas with bodies fitted at Eastern Coach Works (ECW) as replacements for unreliable Guy Wulfrunians. In 1970-72, 39 single-deck Bristol REs were purchased, also with ECW bodies, so it was no surprise when new VR chassis (Vertical Rear-engined) were purchased from 1972 to 1978. Seen before they ever graced the roads of West Yorkshire are two of the batch delivered in autumn 1974. They are proudly carrying the relatively new red livery introduced by the National Bus Company. Although they have West Riding fleet names their eponymous county had been dissolved in April with local government reorganisation and boundary changes. Nos.746 and 744 are having final checks carried out at Eastern Coach Works in Lowestoft before delivery, and will go on to be registered GUA 381N and GUA 379N respectively.

Huddersfield trolleybus No.625 (KVH 225), a 1956 East Lancs H72R-bodied BUT 9641T, in the late afternoon of 26 November 1966. It is not far off the shortest day, so the Waterloo terminus is already shrouded in darkness. The bus is waiting to travel westwards for two miles into the town centre and steadily uphill for four more miles until it reaches the UK's highest trolleybus terminus. This was at Outlane on the edge of the moors, 909 feet above sea level. The system came to an end on Saturday 13 July 1968 when service 73 was the last trolleybus route to operate in Huddersfield. The shiny underside of the copper overhead wires can clearly be seen reflecting the streetlights behind the trolley-booms on the roof of the bus. Mitchell Avenue is the location of this view; at the bottom of the hill, beyond the bus, is the depot of County Motors of Lepton which would merge with Yorkshire Traction in 1969.

In the 1960s car ownership was at a far lower level than is the case today. Doncaster St Leger race meeting used to attract several hundred buses and coaches. In September 1968 a smartly presented 1956 Roe B44F-bodied AEC Reliance MU2RA No.12 (LVH 12) belonging to Huddersfield Joint Omnibus Committee has made its way to the Belle Vue coach park bringing punters to watch England's oldest classic horse race. The sticker in the top of the windscreen shows that it is 'On hire to Hanson'. Hanson's Buses Ltd had been a famous independent operator based in Huddersfield until it sold out in 1969. Huddersfield Joint Omnibus Committee then bought the firm. The coach side of the business was flourishing when West Yorkshire Passenger Transport Executive purchased it in 1974. The double-decker to the left is an Alexander-bodied Leyland Atlantean PDR1/3 owned by East Midland Motor Services Ltd.

No.255 (RJX 255) is an Albion Nimbus N53AN bought new by Halifax Joint Omnibus Committee in 1963. It carries a Weymann B31F body and is one of a batch of ten vehicles. Halifax is associated with woollen mills and industrial premises but, as can be seen, their buses travelled to the most rural of destinations. This is Mill Bank at the terminus of a journey from Halifax on Saturday 22 November 1966. It has travelled via Sowerby Bridge, deep in the Calder Valley, finally climbing high on to the edge of the moors. The bus is fitted with a 4-cylinder Albion engine and a 6-speed crash gearbox that will have taxed the skills of the driver on the final approach, with hills as steep as 1 in 6 to ascend. These troublesome little buses were to be short-lived and this one, renumbered 355 shortly before disposal, was sold off within a year. In 1971 the whole route pattern of services to Mill Bank would change, following the absorption of Hebble Motor Services by Halifax Corporation.

Dennis started to produce its Loline chassis in 1958. It was very similar to the Bristol Lodekka but was available to any purchaser, unlike the Bristol product that was restricted to state-owned companies. 240 were produced until the final five were delivered to Halifax Joint Omnibus Committee (JOC) in 1967. Numerically No.304 (FCP 304E) is the very last vehicle, a Loline III with a Northern Counties H73F body. All five buses were equipped with 5-speed semi-automatic gearboxes and Gardner 6LX engines and were renowned for being fast and powerful. No.304 was only a few weeks old on 13 May 1967 when loading passengers in Halifax. Note the cobblestones on Alexandra Street, still in situ in 2008. However, the Dolphin, a high quality fish restaurant well-loved by local residents, subsequently became the Three Lanterns and is now an Indian restaurant. The bus is ready to make its journey to Huddersfield, on route 43. This service was jointly operated with the Huddersfield Joint Omnibus Committee. After just three years in service these buses were sold to West Riding Automobile Company where they helped to replace unreliable Guy Wulfrunians and continued in service until the late 1970s. In 1971 Halifax JOC merged with Todmorden to form Calderdale JOC but in 1974 the West Yorkshire Passenger Transport Executive swallowed up the whole operation.

In the spring of 1969 an ex-Darlington trolleybus is loading outside the Bradford City Transport (BCT) offices on Bolton Road in the city centre. It is a Karrier W built in 1944 and when in the North East ran as a centre-entrance single-decker. Bradford bought No.786 (GHN 563) and eight others from the batch and in 1958/59 had them fitted with East Lancs H70F bodies. They all ran until 1971 with the exception of No.786, withdrawn in July 1970. To turn round to this position the bus has just travelled round Balme Street and Canal Road, passing the Grattons building (famed for its armchair catalogue shopping) behind the BCT offices. The modern office buildings of Forster Square can be seen to the rear, but the station bearing that name is out of sight a few hundred yards to the right. The rear-engined bus is one of a batch of 20 Alexander-bodied Daimler Fleetlines, with G-registrations, delivered in 1968 and is only a few months old. To the left is No.209 (6209 KW), one of 30 AEC Regent V 2D3RAs delivered in 1964 with Metro-Cammell H40/30F bodies. This brought the total of such vehicles to over 100, some of which were used as early trolleybus replacements.

Llanelly and District became part of South Wales Transport in 1952 and this BET Company quickly closed their trolleybus system down. Bradford purchased ten 1945/46 Karrier Ws from South Wales and had them rebuilt by East Lancs with H35/28R bodies, entering service in their new northern home in 1956. No.775 (CBX 530) is at Thackley Corner halfway between Saltaire and the city centre, a few weeks before its withdrawal on 31 May 1969. The circuitous route took 6½ miles to join the two termini as opposed to the four miles direct to Saltaire. At one time, the turning circle behind the bus was used for regular 41 route short workings but towards the end served merely for early morning and late night turn-backs. Trolleybuses on the 40 route were provided by the depot at Bolton (a suburb of Bradford) until it closed in 1958. The crews and buses for the service 40 to Saltaire and 42 to Greengates, which diverged at Five Lane Ends, were moved to Thornbury depot. For many years after the closure of their home depot the so-called 'Bolton rota' crews continued to operate only on these routes. The whole section was converted to diesel bus operation on 1 July 1971, less than a year before Bradford closed down the last trolleybus system in the UK, on 7 March 1972.

Saltaire depot was one of several owned by Bradford Corporation Transport as they favoured operating a number of smaller suburban garages rather than having one large central base. Until 1963 Saltaire, on the north-west of the city, was responsible for operating the seven mile trolleybus route out to Cross Flatts via Bingley. This was converted to motorbuses but Saltaire was still on a longer, indirect route to the city, via Shipley, Thackley, Idle and Bolton. Trolleybuses normally turned round to head back to the city using the traffic island to the right of this view, but a loop of overhead was maintained through the depot for use in emergencies. The presence of No.832 (LHN 782) would not be normal in this 1970 view, that has captured an intriguing collection of buses spanning several generations. The trolleybus is a third-hand vehicle, a BUT 9611T; it had operated in original condition for Darlington from 1949 to 1952 and then for Doncaster from 1952 to 1959. Bradford bought the batch of six buses and removed the original East Lancs rear entrance bodies replacing five of them with new East Lancs H37/29F coachwork that enabled them to see another nine years of service from 1962 to 1971. Immediately behind is an all-Leyland PD2/3 dating from 1949. It is No.573 (EKY 573) the last in the batch of twenty buses and will have served its city for a creditable 22 years when withdrawn in 1971.

Pennine Motors Ltd of Gargrave had an unusual livery of orange and black. Its operating territory encompassed some of England's most spectacular scenery, in the high Pennines, as the name would suggest. Passengers normally enjoyed the luxury of dual-purpose vehicles on the relatively lengthy journey from Skipton. The main line of the route went via Settle and Ingleton and across into Lancaster, a 43 mile service jointly operated with Ribble Motor Services. UWX 277 is a Leyland Tiger Cub PSUC1/1 built in 1958 and fitted with a Duple Donington DP43F body, a product of their East Midlands works in Loughborough. The bus is negotiating the narrow bridge in the centre of Clapham village, halfway between Settle and its final destination of Ingleton. The signpost on the right points to Clapham station. In 2008 it still boasts a train service but with five departures each way per day it is a little less intensive than its better-known namesake in the suburbs of the capital! The workman has abandoned his sweeping brush by the finger post in favour of studying something of greater interest, on the other side of the river.

In February 1974, just weeks before it was taken over by the West Yorkshire Passenger Transport Executive (WYPTE), Leeds City Transport purchased a solitary Leyland National. It was No.1301 (SUA 301M) and although delivered with 52 bus seats, within a short time they were changed to 48 high-backed seats, the headrests being visible through the bus windows. It was to be another six years before WYPTE bought a further batch of Leyland Nationals in 1980. No.1301 was sometimes used on private hire duties and is on an excursion to York, just over 20 miles from Leeds. It would eventually be converted to a dual-door layout with 26 seats and several wheelchair spaces for welfare work. The historic architecture for which York is famous is particularly lacking in this 1975 view. Redfearn National Glass Limited forms the backdrop. This large factory is just beyond the River Fosse that flows behind the coaches. The red Duple-bodied coach to the right is Doncaster Corporation Transport No.21 (XTG 389H). It came to them from Bebbs of Llantwit Fadre in 1971 and is a 1970 Ford R226 with Duple Viceroy C53F bodywork.

Yorkshire Woollen District buses did not carry their full fleet name; they always proclaimed themselves simply as 'Yorkshire'. The company name continued for several years after the National Bus Company era, until gradually being absorbed into the 'West Riding Group' based in Wakefield rather than their Dewsbury headquarters. The final batch of double-deck buses in traditional red livery comprised 12 ECW H43/31F-bodied Daimler Fleetlines delivered in 1972. No.705 (LHD 315K) was the final vehicle in the batch and is at the western extremity of the company's operating area. It is laying-over in Manchester, Lower Moseley Street bus station, before making its way back over the Pennines to Bradford via Halifax. This route was normally operated by single-deckers and it was unusual to see a double-decker on the service. The X12 route was at one time jointly operated with the much-lamented North Western Road Car Company. The bus station has disappeared in modern times to be replaced by the Bridgewater Hall. To the left, the glass-roofed arch belongs to the one-time Manchester Central Station, closed in 1969 and reopened in 1986 as the G-Mex exhibition centre.

At first glance a Lincolnshire Road Car Company (LRCC) bus would appear to be misplaced in a book about Yorkshire. Goole was on the very edge of the West Riding and was close to the Lincolnshire boundary. Reliance of Stainforth, West Riding Automobile and East Yorkshire Motor Services provided long distance routes to this inland port but the town service was provided by a handful of buses from a 'Road Car' depot in Burlington Crescent. This depot was acquired in 1950 with the take-over of the 150-strong Enterprise & Silver Dawn Company, along with a service from Goole to Scunthorpe. Many areas served by 'Road Car' were flat so the company was a regular purchaser of the lightweight Bristol SC4LK (Small Capacity) with an ECW 35 seat body. The bus is powered by a relatively small Gardner 4LK engine with only four cylinders and a capacity of 3.8 litres, linked to a crash-gearbox. No.2494 (RFE 482) is heading from the garage to the town centre terminus and is attempting to travel incognito with all the destinations blanked off. This vehicle is a relatively late member of its class. Lincolnshire Road Car bought over 100 of these buses between 1956 and 1961 and this one was delivered in the final batch. As a final survivor it was of a limited number to carry NBC style fleet names on the roof panels. By chance this bus would go on to be preserved by LRCC in 1988 and restored to its original condition. The vehicle behind the bus is a three-wheel invalid carriage of a type built in the 1960s and 1970s.

Hull Corporation Transport No.191 (7391 RH) is one of 195 Leyland Atlanteans bought between 1960 and 1975. Along with the majority of them, it carries a Roe body, in this case seating 75 passengers. It is one of the early conversions enabling 'pay-as-you-enter' operation as shown by the rectangular sign over the nearside headlight. The conversion programme commenced in 1969 and involved the use of fare-boxes with no change given. Hull buses were always notable for having a prominent route number display and just a small aperture showing either the destination or a 'via' screen showing the main road traversed by the bus. A large orange sign can be seen behind the bus bearing the legend 'Hull Corporation Pier'. This belonged to British Railways North Eastern Region and was one of a handful of stations in England that never saw a train! (Dartmouth for Kingswear in Devon was another example.) Until the Humber Bridge opened in 1981 this was the terminal for the paddle steamers crossing to New Holland in Lincolnshire. The little trolleys behind the bus carry goods for transit and will be towed by a small tug down the linkspan and on to the deck of the ferry. The VW Transporter is in a designated waiting area and will soon be on board *Lincoln*, *Tattershall* or *Wingfield Castle* to make the 20 minute voyage across to Lincolnshire.

East Yorkshire Motor Services (EYMS) was part of the British Electric Traction group but always had its own unique character. This was because of its unusual dark blue livery and, of course, the unique Beverley Bar roof profile. This was a feature of nearly all their double-deck buses until 1958. The height restriction sign at the Beverley Bar, a Gothic arch, proclaimed it as just 10 feet 9 inches; at this time it spanned a main route out of the town and the safest option was to have all buses in the area built to a shape that would fit through it. A 30ft long AEC Regent V LD3RV with a Roe H34/32RD body, No.651 (WAT 651) was one of a pair delivered in 1958, the last two highbridge buses delivered to EYMS with fully doomed roofs. The location of this view, taken on 23 October 1966, is Bridlington bus station. This was a fine 1930s building providing full facilities for the passengers and staff alike. It would be replaced by a small bay with a few bus shelters when demolished to make way for the Promenades Shopping Centre at the end of the 1990s. Just to the rear is one of 15 Willowbrook 56-seat AEC Regent V MD3RVs with 27 foot bodies, delivered in 1956.

East Yorkshire had a preference for AEC double-deckers throughout the period from 1956 to 1966. As low-height buses were developed, the company bought several batches of AEC Bridgemasters and then AEC Renowns. It was discovered that even these lower vehicles would only fit through Beverley Bar if the top deck of the body was tapered inwards. This feature can be seen on No.784 (CKH 784C) a 1965 AEC Renown 3B3RA with Park Royal H40/30F bodywork. To the left is No.844 (PKH 844G), a rear-engined Leyland Panther Cub PSRC1/1, dating from 1968 and fitted with a Marshall B45F body. It is the autumn of 1974 soon after the company had started painting its buses in National Bus Company poppy red. This was a major contrast with the old blue livery seen on the two buses behind. No.844 continued in service until 1978, but No.784 lasted longer, becoming a driver-training vehicle in 1979. An interesting list of potential destinations appears on the wall above the Panther Cub.

Wallace Arnold (WA) was well known as a coach operator. It also ran stage carriage services in three areas of Yorkshire, two near Leeds and one in Scarborough. Two companies owned by WA, Kippax and District Motors and the Farsley Omnibus Company of Pudsey, were sold off to Leeds Corporation in 1968 but Hardwick's of Scarborough, in the North Riding, continued operating into the 1980s. In 1971 four AEC Swifts were acquired to operate their route from Scarborough to Ebberston via various delightfully named villages as shown on the destination blind of TWE 22F. These buses were bought by Sheffield Transport in 1968, part of a batch of 20 vehicles fitted with Park Royal B49D bodies. The rest continued in service with South Yorkshire PTE, the successors to Sheffield Transport, until the late 1970s. Ex-Sheffield No.22 is parked at the bus station at Westwood, Scarborough, which is the terminal point of the route. Four Leyland Leopards replaced the AECs three years later. These new vehicles had locally built Plaxton Panorama coach bodies but were fitted with ordinary bus seats. Wallace Arnold and its subsidiaries used this grey and orange livery for a period, replacing their traditional cream livery of the fifties, only to re-introduce the cream livery in later years. Hardwick's would eventually be sold to East Yorkshire Motor Services in 1987.

Valley Bridge bus station in Scarborough was a magnet for Tilling Group Bristol/ECW vehicles. At first glance there are a number of near identical buses, but closer inspection shows many variations. The three most prominent vehicles are Bristol RE (Rear-Engined) buses. Each one is fitted with an ECW body and, by chance, the three main different types of front end and windscreen are to be seen. The unidentified bus on the left, the last style to be produced from 1970 onwards with a BET-style curved glass windscreen, is owned by the West Yorkshire Road Car Company based in Harrogate. They had a small garage and depot at Northway, Scarborough until the end of the 1960s. After this closed, their handful of buses was stabled at United's Vernon Road garage. This West Yorkshire Bristol RE has travelled 44 miles from York, on the 43 route. Some journeys on this service were extended as far as Leeds and Bradford. The other two REs are home-based United vehicles, the one in the middle, No.4123 (AHN 623B) is a RELL6G, an early design with a two-leaf door and narrow entrance and a windscreen curved only at the outside edges. In 1962, when first introduced, this was a very modern development. This bus has arrived from Bridlington on route 12, a service which would eventually be amalgamated with East Yorkshire's similar, competing, route. No.4188 (THN 888F) dating from 1968 is another RELL6G operating the local route 114 to Cloughton. This RE has an intermediate design of flat windscreen. The slightly shy Bristol MW (Medium Weight) also belongs to United and is a dual-purpose vehicle acting as a duplicate on route 43.

United Automobile Services had its head office in Darlington but covered an area stretching over 100 miles, from Bridlington to Berwick-upon-Tweed. No.U277 (277 EHN) is a 1957 Bristol LS5G with ECW B45F bodywork, slogging its way out of Sandsend, just north of Whitby. The bus is climbing Lythe Bank with its maximum gradient of 1 in 4. With only 7.0 litres and 94 horsepower at its disposal No.U277 is making slow but steady progress having made a compulsory stop at the bottom of the bank to engage first gear. The valley in the background carries the Mickleby Beck out to the North Sea, just a few hundred yards to the left. Until 1958 a railway line also ran from Whitby to Middlesbrough, sweeping over the valley 60ft up, on a distinctive eight-span metal viaduct alongside the seafront. Many of United's services ran up and down similar gradients in the North Yorkshire Moors and the Cleveland Hills but, surprisingly, nearly all of its single-deck fleet was fitted with the low powered Gardner 5-cylinder engine rather than the 6-cylinder equivalent.

In the north of the county a Teesside Municipal Transport trolleybus is pulling into the bus stop alongside its depot at South Bank just to the east of Middlesbrough. No.T291 (VRD 186) is a relative stranger to the area, having been built for Reading Transport in 1961 and then moving to Teesside in 1969 following the closure of its home system in November 1968. Five of these modern H68F Burlingham-bodied Sunbeam F4As made their way north and two of them gave service until closure of the Teesside system on 4 April 1971. No.T291 was chosen to be the 'last' trolleybus and was painted in a special livery, commemorating 52 years of trolleybus service, from 1919 to 1971. On the final afternoon it was the last vehicle in an official procession and carried a civic party. Teesside Municipal Transport was the UK's penultimate trolleybus operator. The unusual abbreviated destination N B Y indicates to locals that the bus will travel to Eston anti-clockwise round the loop via Normanby. Grangetown on the eastern side of the circuit would be similarly shown as G T N. On this cold winter day just before the demise of the trolleybuses, there will be few takers for the passing United Automobile Bristol MW, which is travelling from Middlesbrough to the coastal town of Redcar, eight miles away.

Charles Roe of Leeds was the last coachbuilder in the UK to produce significant numbers of bodies for trolleybuses. They developed a standard body for fitting on refurbished trolleybus chassis and supplied them to operators including Ashton-under-Lyne, Doncaster, Maidstone, Wolverhampton and the Tees-side Railless Traction Board. Tees-side had their entire fleet of fifteen trolleybuses re-bodied between 1960 and 1965, No.5 (GAJ 15) being the last one. It was renumbered T285 in August 1970 and carried this identity for less than a year until the system closed in April 1971. The trolleybuses were housed in a covered part of the depot visible just behind the siding where No.T285 is parked. The new authority dropped the hyphen in Tees-side used by its predecessor and the fleet name 'Teesside Municipal Transport', dating back to the April 1968 re-organisation, is on the white band between the decks. There are indications of the industrial nature of this area behind the bus, where part of the Cargo Fleet Iron Works stands alongside the office block of its parent company, Dorman Long.

From 1957 to 1967 Tees-side Railless Traction Board (TRTB) standardised on Roe-bodied Leyland PD2s for its motor bus purchases. The earlier ones had 'Midland Red' style 'tin fronts' whilst the later ones were fitted with 'St Helens' style fibreglass fronts. One of the latter is seen at its home depot on a grey winter day in 1971. The original dark green livery of TRTB has been replaced by the turquoise introduced following the formation of Teesside Municipal Transport in April 1968. This followed the combining of several local authorities including Eston UDC, which owned two thirds of TRTB, Middlesbrough Corporation who ran a fleet of buses in blue livery and Stockton Corporation, which had a dark green fleet. No.H239 (FVN 39D), a Roe H33/28R-bodied Leyland PD2A/27 is alongside the offices of its former owner at South Bank. The twin louvres next to the destination box show that the bus is fitted with Cave-Brown-Cave heating. This relatively unusual system involved additional radiators, shutters and extraction ducts behind the visible grills. This area has extensive iron and steel works, and is also well known for its chemical industry. This is reflected in the destination 'ICI WILTON', a large plant to the east of Middlesbrough. The peeling advertisement on the side of the bus is for Teesside Park Racecourse, Stockton, which would be closed in 1981 and eventually covered by the Teesside shopping centre in 1989.

The York Pullman Bus Co Ltd was a small but proud operator of an immaculate fleet based in the centre of Yorkshire's county town. Unusually, their head office was in a 13th Century gatehouse, Bootham Tower, close to York's famous Minster. The purpose-built depot was just by the city wall at Navigation Road and, as can be seen, was a substantial building. It was capable of holding the entire fleet of about twenty vehicles. No.77 (9677 DN), a 1964 AEC Regent V 2MD3RA with Roe H37/28RD bodywork, is taking a rest between duties on a Saturday afternoon in 1970. The advertisement on the side of the bus is hand painted and is promoting York Pullman's own coaches. This fine vehicle would go on to give fifteen years of service until withdrawal in January 1979. The company would go through several changes of ownership before finally closing down in 1990. This famous name and livery refused to die and has been revived in 2007 by a new operator. The Navigation Road depot is still there but, sadly, is used as a car park.

York Pullman operated services to several rural destinations around the city. These included Helperby, Easingwold and Stamford Bridge. No.72 (SDN 787), a 1959 AEC Reliance 2MU3RV with a Roe C41F body, is heading back towards its base late in the afternoon on a Saturday in autumn 1970. When it was first delivered the yellow relief continued round the beading on to the front of the vehicle. This gave it a more coach-like appearance. It is en route from the delightfully named Holme-upon-Spalding Moor back to York Piccadilly. It will arrive in the city after the shops have closed so there are few passengers wishing to make use of the service. The destination blinds for the outward journey on this route were abbreviated and vehicles would announce themselves as simply going to 'Holme' when home was really back in York!

In the twenty years since the de-regulation of bus services, the face of sightseeing services has changed completely. In 1967 when this bus was plying its trade, open top buses were mainly seen on the sunny south coast of England. In the year 2008, most city tours will have open top double-deckers driving round in all weathers, often with passengers huddling under umbrellas! Not so in the 1960s: one solitary Bedford OB with classic Duple C26F body in the York-West Yorkshire fleet was more than adequate for the demand. A large percentage of York's visitors would be made up of native Yorkshire folk paying homage to their county town and its fine Minster. As No.CP1 (Coach, Petrol) (FWW 596) waits near York railway station, it seems to have more than enough capacity on this late summer day as it attempts to attract customers for its City Tour. This duty was allocated to a regular driver with much local knowledge. The coach was one of four delivered in 1947. When chosen for the role of a sightseeing vehicle it had additional quarter light windows added above the normal side windows. Happily it would survive after withdrawal to be preserved and live on into the next century. York was at the focal point of the three Ridings yet, as such, the city was not in of any of them.